Contents

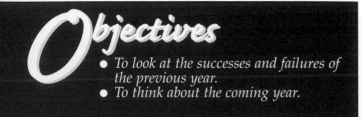
Moving forward

CONSIDER

1. Make a list of all your achievements over the last year. These may be things you did in or out of school. Which achievement are you most proud of? Why?

2. Darren and Kim are thinking about things that they did not do well last year. Which one is being honest? Which one has learned and is likely to change?

> My mum was cross with my Geography report because it said I hadn't worked hard. I DID do some work, and anyway, it was the teacher's fault. He didn't like me, he always picked on me in class and the work was too hard. You can't work well if you don't like the teacher.

> I was in a lot of trouble last year because I showed off in class and was cheeky to a new teacher. I did it to get a laugh but I was sent out so much that I fell behind in the lesson. It seemed funny at the time but really it's me that has suffered because now I've been put in a lower Maths group. I'm going to have to work hard this year if I'm going to be ready to start the exam course next year.

3. Think about the things you did last year that were not successful. Be honest with yourself. What went wrong? Why did it happen? What did you learn from it?

FACT TO THINK ABOUT ... FACT TO THINK ABOUT ... FACT TO THINK ABOUT ...

Many teachers feel that this school year is the one when pupils are most likely to go 'off the rails' as far as work and behaviour are concerned.

KEY WORDS   achievements   strengths   weaknesses   success   failure

4. Now look at your achievements and successes and think about the skills involved, or lacking, in each one. Draw two charts like the one below, showing skills you have and skills you need to learn. The chart below only shows one success and one failure but you should include more.

Successes	Skills learned
played in netball team	teamwork, commitment, perseverance
Failures	**Skills needed**
argued with parents nearly every day	tolerance, thinking about other people's points of view, the ability to talk through problems

5. Write a statement about what you want to achieve this year in and out of school and say why these things are important to you.

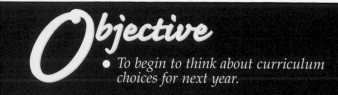

Objective

• *To begin to think about curriculum choices for next year.*

Which subjects?

1. If you had a completely free choice of which subjects to study and which ones to drop, what would you choose? Give reasons for your choice.

2. Schools often use the phrase 'a broad and balanced curriculum'. What do you think this means? Is it important?

3. At this stage in your schooling, you may be asked to make choices in the near future. These might be about which subjects to take and which subjects to drop, what level to study certain subjects at, what examinations to take or whether to include some vocational, basic skills or social skills subjects.
What choices will you have to make? Make a list of the subjects you will have to take next year, then list all the other subjects or courses you need to make a decision about.

4. Kathy is using a diagram to help her decide which subjects to choose next year. She has written the 'pros' in one colour and the 'cons' in another. Not all Kathy's comments are very helpful. Which comments should she ignore when making her decision?

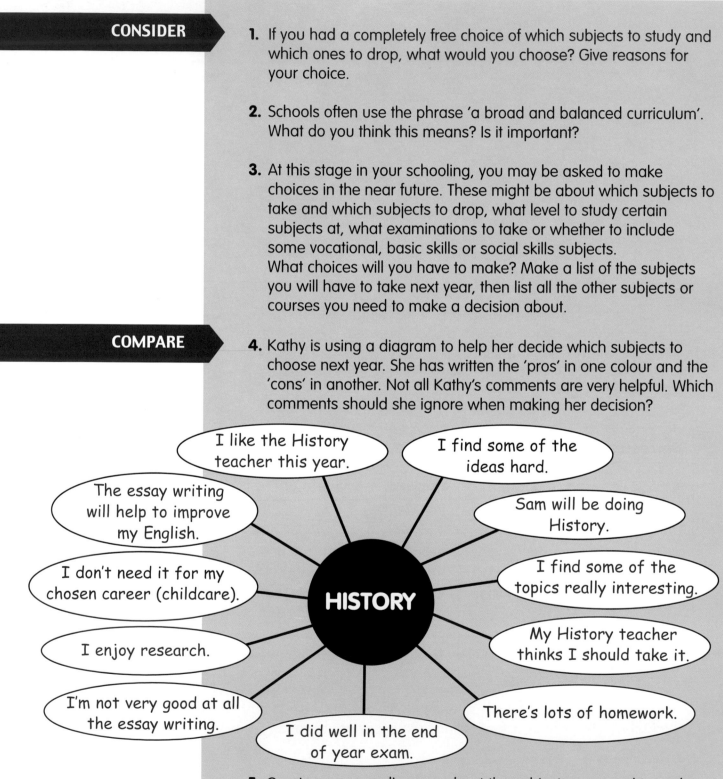

5. Create your own diagram about the subjects you need to make choices in.

FACT TO THINK ABOUT ... FACT TO THINK ABOUT ... FACT TO THINK ABOUT ...

The National Curriculum was introduced in England and Wales in 1988 and was the first UK Act to set out in detail what should be taught in schools.

KEY WORDS | curriculum   options   choices

6. Sometimes, choices made at this stage can limit choices later on, although there is usually a way round it if you are really determined. Read the comments below.

> I dropped Art when I was 15 because I was useless at painting. Then I became interested in textiles and wanted to do an Art foundation course before going on to do clothes design. I wrote a letter to the college explaining the problem and put together a portfolio of work I'd created in my spare time. I did get a place but it would have been much easier if I'd taken Art.

> I took French but I dropped German even though I was good at it. Now I'm doing a secretarial course and my tutor says I should specialise in languages. I'm going to sign up for an evening class in German next year.

7. Now write down the choices you think you might make. (This doesn't have to be your final decision.) Will this choice close any options to you later on? Is this likely to be a problem?

CONSIDER

8. Although the final decision will be yours, you might find it useful to talk things over with teachers, parents, careers or personal advisers or other students who have taken particular subjects. Make a list of people you might want to talk to about the choices you need to make and write down any questions you might want to ask.

PLAN

Objective
● To relate job opportunities to personal skills, strengths and aptitudes.

Which job?

CONSIDER

1. Write down a list of at least ten jobs you definitely would not want to do. Do they have anything in common? What is it about these jobs that puts you off?

2. Now you have the harder task of thinking about what you would like to do. Most people are happier in a job if they feel they are good at it. This means you need to choose work that will use your skills. Make a list of your skills. The pictures below may give you some ideas, but there are plenty of others as well.

Solving problems	Working alone	Working as a team	Coping with new situations
Using figures	Listening	Doing practical work	Being creative

IMAGINE

3. Working in small groups, take it in turns to suggest jobs. Each time a job is suggested, imagine that you have just been told you will have to do that job. What is your immediate reaction? What one thing do you think you might like about the job? What one thing would you dislike? Keep going until you have considered about ten jobs. Write down anything you have discovered about types of work you would or would not like to do.

FACT TO THINK ABOUT ... FACT TO THINK ABOUT ... FACT TO THINK ABOUT ...

A qualification, at whatever level, cannot guarantee you a job, but surveys show that, on average, better qualified people earn more money than those without qualifications.

KEY WORDS | skills   strengths   employability   qualification

4. Think about the atmosphere you would like to work in. Which of the situations below would suit you? What else would you look for in your ideal work atmosphere?

CONSIDER

Working outdoors	Challenging work with tight deadlines and important decisions	Feeling you are helping someone
Working with other people	Being in authority	Being with others your own age

5. Chris has done all the activities above and now has an idea about what he would and would not like to do, although he does not yet have a particular job in mind. Read Chris's statement. What jobs might suit this profile?

6. Write a statement like Chris's, summing up the kind of work you would and would not like to do. Show your statement to other people and ask them to suggest jobs that might fit your profile.

> I'd like to work indoors, where the work is fairly predictable and I know what I'm doing. I don't mind working hard, but I don't want a very stressful job with lots of decisions. I'd like to work with a small group of other people, but not have to deal with members of the public or lots of people I don't know. I don't want to do anything too messy or involving lifting and carrying, but I'd quite like to work with my hands or machinery. I want a regular nine-to-five job, no weekends.

Objective
● To understand the role of personal advisers and how they can help young people.

Getting help with your future

1. Make a list of things you might need advice on over the next few years. (Hint: think about school, relationships, yourself and your plans for the future.) When you have written your list, note down people or places you could go to for advice on each item.

CONSIDER

2. Personal advisers are the people who provide advice and help for young people at school and afterwards. An important part of their role is to advise young people about careers, training and education, but they are also there to advise or listen to problems about relationships, sex and any other matters of concern. Think about the sort of person who would make a good personal adviser. Write a 'person specification' describing the skills, experience and training a good personal adviser would need.

PLAN

3. Imagine you are a personal adviser. The following young people, Liam, Raji, Becky and Tim, have come to see you. What things would you ask them? Write an action plan for each one showing the advice you would give and suggesting things you and the young person could do to tackle the issue.

I'm fed up with school but I'm quite clever and my parents and teachers all expect me to stay on for the sixth form.

I want to work with animals.

Liam   Raji

FACT TO THINK ABOUT ... FACT TO THINK ABOUT ... FACT TO THINK ABOUT ...

There are about 20 000 types of work and these can be sub-divided into hundreds of different jobs.

KEY WORDS | personal adviser | career | personal specification

Becky   Tim

4. Jodie has no idea what she wants to do when she leaves school. Brian wants to be a dentist but he doesn't know what training or qualifications he will need or how to apply. Draw two spider charts, one for Jodie and one for Brian, showing the people they could talk to, the resources they could use and any other actions they need to take.

Jodie

Brian

5. You may be like Jodie and have no idea what you want to do when you leave school, or you may have some ideas. Draw your own spider chart showing what you could do, who you could talk to and where you could look in order to develop your career plans.

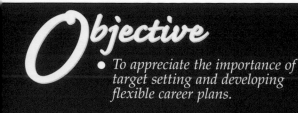

Objective
• To appreciate the importance of target setting and developing flexible career plans.

Target setting and career plans

1. The students below are writing 'wish lists' showing things they would like to have in their adult lives. Write your own wish list of ten things you would like to have, which you realistically think you might stand a chance of getting if you work for them.

CONSIDER

2. Now look at your list and work out the costs involved. What kind of wages will you need in order to pay for it all? What kind of jobs would pay these wages? It might help to look at job advertisements in local or national newspapers.

3. Over the next few years, you will probably find that plenty of people give you advice about career plans. Unfortunately, the advice is often conflicting – 'aim high/know your limits', 'work towards one aim/keep your options open', 'take opportunities when they arise/make your own chances'. Probably the best advice is to have a career plan, but be prepared to alter it if you or your circumstances change. Look at the two plans on the next page. What are the strengths and possible weaknesses of each plan?

Some people find that, although they are unable to achieve their original career plan, they can adapt it in some way. For example, Jo got a job doing shift work in a factory and, on her mornings off, worked as a volunteer at a primary school. Eventually she was offered a full-time post as a classroom assistant.

KEY WORDS   career targets   lifestyle   plan

FRANCES' CAREER PLAN

Personal profile:
good with children, calm, artistic, quiet but with a strong personality.

Career aim:
nursery nurse.

Next step after school:
two year NNEB course.

Next step after training:
to get a job working with children in a nursery or similar place.

Future plans:
to take a Business Studies course as an evening class while working, so as to have a better chance of eventually becoming a manager of a nursery unit.

TYRONE'S CAREER PLAN

Personal profile:
slight learning difficulties, good with people, likes working in the open air and growing things, strong and not afraid of hard work.

Career aim:
gardener.

Subject options:
key skills course that includes extra work on social and basic skills, and a work placement for one day a week. Choice for work placement – garden centre.

Next step after school:
two years at horticultural college.

Next step after training:
work for private firm or local authority in parks and gardens.

Future plans:
evening class.

4. Write your own career plan. You may need to find out about option choices in your school, and about training and qualifications needed for your chosen career. If you have no idea what you want to do yet, write a plan for a job you could imagine yourself doing. Writing the plan may help to clarify things you do or don't want to do.

PLAN

5. Now use your career plan to set yourself targets. What do you need to do this year towards achieving your career aim? What do you need to have done by the time you leave school?

CONSIDER

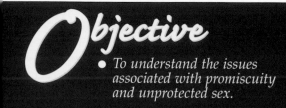

Objective

● To understand the issues associated with promiscuity and unprotected sex.

CONSIDER

1. Which of the following definitions are correct?
   a. Promiscuous means:
      i) having many casual sexual relationships
      ii) having sex many times with one person
      iii) only having sex when you are married.
   b. Monogamous means:
      i) not having sex
      ii) having only one married partner at a time
      iii) having many wives or husbands.
   c. Celibate means:
      i) only having sex with your husband or wife
      ii) not having sex
      iii) enjoying sex.
   d. Unprotected sex means:
      i) having sex under 16
      ii) having sex with someone you don't know
      iii) having sex without using a condom or femidom.
   e. A sexually transmitted infection (STI) is:
      i) any infection affecting the genital area
      ii) AIDS
      iii) any infection passed on through sexual contact.

2. Look at the figures below and think about what each one means. What do they suggest about the sexual behaviour of boys, girls and adults in the last few years?

- In 1998, more than 1200 girls and 191 boys under the age of 16 sought medical help for sexually transmitted infections.
- The number of girls under 16 being treated for STIs has risen by over 65 per cent in eight years, the increase for boys under 16 has been just four per cent.
- Cases of gonorrhoea in all age groups rose by 25 per cent last year, with over 15 570 sufferers.
- Cases of gonorrhoea among teenage boys rose by nearly 40 per cent. Cases among teenage girls rose by 24 per cent. Experts believe the difference between boys and girls may be explained by the fact that up to 80 per cent of female carriers may not realise they are carrying the disease.
- Doctors treating patients with STIs are frustrated by the fact that many of their patients return several times with new infections. One GP said, "Young people may come in four or five times, each time with a new infection. The safer sex message just isn't getting across."

FACT TO THINK ABOUT ... FACT TO THINK ABOUT ... FACT TO THINK ABOUT ...

When one group of university students was asked about their first sexual experience, 62 per cent said they hadn't enjoyed it.

KEY WORDS sexually transmitted infection   promiscuous   unprotected sex   sexual activity

3. How can you definitely avoid catching a sexually transmitted infection? How can you reduce the risk of catching one?

4. Read the comments below. Where do you think the message to start having sex early comes from? Is it the same for boys and girls? Do young people who have sex do it because they want to or because they feel they should?

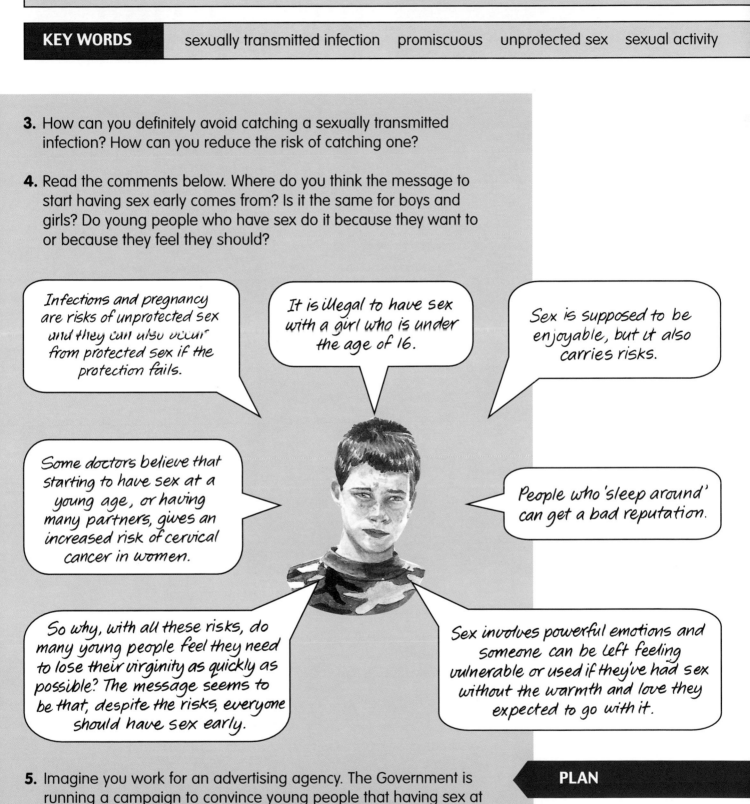

Infections and pregnancy are risks of unprotected sex and they can also occur from protected sex if the protection fails.

It is illegal to have sex with a girl who is under the age of 16.

Sex is supposed to be enjoyable, but it also carries risks.

Some doctors believe that starting to have sex at a young age, or having many partners, gives an increased risk of cervical cancer in women.

People who 'sleep around' can get a bad reputation.

So why, with all these risks, do many young people feel they need to lose their virginity as quickly as possible? The message seems to be that, despite the risks, everyone should have sex early.

Sex involves powerful emotions and someone can be left feeling vulnerable or used if they've had sex without the warmth and love they expected to go with it.

5. Imagine you work for an advertising agency. The Government is running a campaign to convince young people that having sex at an early age isn't necessarily a good thing. They want the advertisements to look at the facts about the dangers of early and unprotected sex, and also to reinforce the message that it can be a good thing to wait until you are older to have sex. Put together a series of advertisements to get these messages across.

PLAN

15

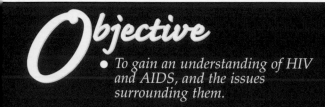

Understanding HIV and AIDS

Objective
● To gain an understanding of HIV and AIDS, and the issues surrounding them.

CONSIDER

1. Answer true or false to the following statements:
   a. HIV is a virus that attacks the immune system. You can be HIV positive for a long time without having any symptoms.
   b. A person with AIDS is someone who is ill as a result of being HIV positive.
   c. In 1998, the biggest group of people contracting the HIV virus was gay men.
   d. Five million children have the HIV virus worldwide.
   e. You can't catch HIV from oral sex.

2. Sort the statements below into two groups headed 'HIV can be passed on this way' and 'HIV cannot be passed on this way'.

vaginal or anal sex without a condom

oral sex

sharing cutlery

sneezing on someone

sharing needles or syringes

using the same flannel

from a mother to a baby during pregnancy, at birth or through breastfeeding

from a blood transfusion in the UK

3. Wendy and her ten-year-old son both have the HIV virus. She campaigns for funding into research and for education to help people understand more about AIDS and HIV. Read her comments:

> People often listen to me because my son and I don't look like 'typical AIDS victims', but every person suffering from AIDS deserves to be treated with compassion. I didn't know I had the HIV virus when I was pregnant – they didn't offer you an HIV test in those days. If I had known, the doctors might have been able to stop my son from contracting it. I don't tell people Josh is HIV positive. He is no risk to them or their children, but I know of children who have been forced to leave school and lost all their friends because parents are scared that their children might catch it just from playing with an HIV carrier.

16

FACT TO THINK ABOUT ... FACT TO THINK ABOUT ... FACT TO THINK ABOUT ...

In the UK, 91 per cent of people think that more education about AIDS and HIV should be given to young people.

KEY WORDS   AIDS   HIV   heterosexual   homosexual   prejudice

4. Gary works as a 'buddy'. This is a volunteer who befriends someone suffering from AIDS and gives them practical and emotional support, often until they die.

> I feel privileged to have helped people suffering from AIDS. They have to cope with prejudice as well as the illness. If someone gets cancer, they are immediately given sympathy and support but if someone develops AIDS, they can face cruel comments or hurtful actions, like people avoiding them.

> I have been visiting AIDS sufferers for over five years. I help them to wash, cook and eat. I've hugged them and sat holding their hands and I know that I'm not at any risk of catching the virus myself. Some people say that AIDS victims deserve the disease because they are gay or drug addicts or something. No one deserves to die just because they may have had unprotected sex or taken other risks. I just wish they hadn't taken the risk in the first place.

ROLE–PLAY

5. Imagine you are either Gary or Wendy. You were due to meet someone for a meal but they cancelled because they found out about your work with AIDS sufferers. In pairs, role-play a telephone conversation where you confront the person about his or her prejudice. What can you say to change that person's mind? Swap roles so that you each get a chance to play Gary or Wendy.

6. Prejudice usually stems from ignorance. Put together a television advert showing the facts about HIV and AIDS, aimed at encouraging people to accept others who are HIV positive into their schools or communities without prejudice.

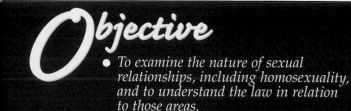

Objective

- To examine the nature of sexual relationships, including homosexuality, and to understand the law in relation to those areas.

Sexuality

CONSIDER

1. Read the comments below. What do they tell you about relationships and sexuality?

> I have had good sexual relationships with men and women but the relationship I'm in now is the best yet. That's not because he's a man - it's just to do with who he is and what he's like.

> My partner and I are very happy. He makes me laugh but we can talk about serious things too. I can't imagine life without him.

> At the moment I'm just not interested in sex. I came out of a relationship quite recently and I don't want to get involved with anyone else for the time being.

> My wife and I have been married for 42 years. Someone asked her recently what the secret of our happy marriage was and she said, "Good sex!" There's more to it than that but it certainly helps.

BRAINSTORM

2. Brainstorm the things that make people happy in a relationship. Do these things apply equally to heterosexual and homosexual relationships?

FACT TO THINK ABOUT ... FACT TO THINK ABOUT ... FACT TO THINK ABOUT ...

In parts of the British Isles, male homosexuals were executed until the eighteenth century.

KEY WORDS | sexuality   homosexual   heterosexual

3. The law on sex is quite confusing. Read the information below. Do you think the law is fair? What changes would you recommend?

CONSIDER

- It is illegal for a male to have sex with a girl who is under the age of 16.
- A woman who has sex with a boy who is under the age of 16 could be prosecuted for indecent assault.
- There is no law stating the age of consent for lesbians, but a woman having sex with a girl under 16 could be prosecuted for indecent assault.
- The age of consent for gay men is 16, and homosexual acts are only legal if both partners consent and the act takes place in private with no one else present.

4. The following poem was written by Sharon, aged 15. At the time, Sharon was wondering about her own sexuality. What do you think Sharon is saying? What emotions do you think she is feeling?

Take your time

See that boy? See that girl? (Take your time – take your time.)
Classroom taunts, "She's a dyke." (Got to laugh, got to hide.)
In the showers, on the bus. See his muscles. See her thigh.
Feelings stir, my hands reach out (take your time, take your time).
One drunk night it all came out. See them stare, hear them gasp.
Tried to take it back – too late. Can't they see I just don't know?
It's like I'm forced to make a choice. Then I heard a voice inside.
Take your time. Take your time.
You've got a lifetime. Take your time.

5. Write a poem or piece of writing about sexuality. It does not need to be about your own sexuality, it could be about an imaginary person, or it could be general advice to young people thinking about their own and other people's sexuality.

*O*bjective

- To look at the nature of the relationship between brothers and sisters and to work out strategies for coping with problems in this area.

Brothers and sisters

1. The statements below were all made by people of your age. Write your own statements about brothers and sisters.

An older sister is someone who knows everything and gets away with everything.

A younger brother is just a pain in the bum!

A younger sister never does anything wrong, and lies through her teeth!

A younger brother is someone who thinks you are really cool!

An older brother looks out for you and never lets you down.

2. Problems between siblings (brothers or sisters) are common. Write replies to some of these letters.

Dear Leah,

My brother is three years older than me. At school, he does no work and is always in trouble. I've been at this school just three weeks and already I'm sick of teachers saying, "Oh, you're Kieran's brother are you?" in a voice that says it all. I've left it too late to change my surname. What should I do?

Gavin

Dear Leah,

I have an older brother and a younger sister and I'm stuck in the middle. When I ask why my brother is allowed to do something, they say, "Well, he's the oldest," and when my sister gets away with stuff, they say, "Well, she's the youngest." What I want to know is, what are the perks of being the middle child?

Sangeeta

20

KEY WORDS   sibling   sibling rivalry   jealousy   love

Dear Leah,

I'm sick of my little sister Melanie. She's five years younger than me, prettier, cleverer and generally nicer, so I'm told. Seriously though, I do feel that she gets all the attention. The other day, my dad was reading a story I'd written at school, when Mel came in. My dad immediately put down the story and hasn't looked at it since. I've left it in the kitchen for three days. I feel like that exercise book. Ignored.

Kim

Dear Leah,

When my brother Jake was born I was twelve and it was very exciting. Since then though, Mum has had twins, Lottie and Sheena, and they are all hard work. Mum expects me to help all the time. I have so much to do that I never get to go out with my friends. I know it's hard for Mum being a single parent with four children but I sometimes think she forgets that I'm a child too. I'm only fifteen.

Max

CONSIDER

3. Some psychologists believe that the position you are brought up in within your family can influence your personality. What are the advantages and disadvantages of being: the oldest, the youngest, one of many, an only child, a twin? Do you think any of these things might affect someone's personality?

4. Some siblings get on very well together, but most siblings fall out at least some of the time, and some siblings argue almost all the time. What advice would you give to someone who really didn't get on with their brother or sister? Is it worth trying to improve the relationship and, if so, how could it be done?

5. Parents can't guarantee that their children will get on well together, but there may be some things they can do that will help. Write an advice sheet for parents, giving ideas for how they could help their children get on well with each other.

A growing concern

CONSIDER

1. Elliot and Lauren both tried to commit suicide but were found in time to be saved. Read their comments, then make a list of the problems that they were facing. What other problems might make a young person feel suicidal?

I used to be a happy person. Even after my parents divorced, things weren't too bad, but then my mum got ill and had to give up work. We had no money and I stopped going into town with my mates because I could never afford to buy lunch or anything. My girlfriend finished with me and I started to skive off school. I got into a lot of trouble but when I went back things got worse. People started picking on me, laughing at my haircut and my clothes. One boy used to punch me every morning on the bus. No one liked me and I thought, what's the point? Every day at the bus stop I would think about how easy it would be to end it all by stepping into the road. One morning I saw this lorry coming towards me and I just stepped out.

Everyone thinks I should be happy. I live in a big house, we have lots of money, I get new clothes and holidays every year. I don't know what's wrong with me. My older sister is always happy. She is clever and very popular at school. Last year I got pregnant. My parents were upset but they didn't kick me out or anything. They arranged for me to have an abortion in a private clinic and no one knew about it. They don't mention it now. I feel like everyone would be better off without me. I took lots of pills but they found me and had my stomach pumped. Now I'm supposed to be grateful.

Objective
● To look at teenage suicide and suicide attempts.

22

FACT TO THINK ABOUT ... FACT TO THINK ABOUT ... FACT TO THINK ABOUT ...

Studies by the Samaritans show that, on average, three young people every hour try to harm themselves or attempt suicide.

KEY WORDS   suicide   self-harm   stress   depression

2. Make a list of the signs that might have shown Elliot's and Lauren's friends and families that they were reaching desperation point.

3. Imagine you were a friend of either Elliot or Lauren. Write two conversations you had with them, one before their suicide attempt and one after it, where you talk about what happened.

IMAGINE

4. Read the comment below. Why is talking about how you feel so important? What makes it difficult to do?

> Everyone gets low sometimes but if you are having suicidal thoughts please, please talk to someone. You may be able to talk to someone in your family, a friend, doctor, teacher or other adult. You could call the Samaritans, which is a phone line for people who are feeling lonely, desperate or suicidal. They also run some drop-in centres. The important thing is to talk to someone.

5. You have been given permission to use the back of a rock concert ticket to print a message that might help someone who is feeling suicidal. The ticket size is a quarter of an A4 sheet. Think about the advice you could give and what you could say that might really help them. Design the back of the ticket.

6. A magazine aimed at teenagers once published an article about how to commit suicide, including advice about ways of doing it. The article also included advice on how to deal with problems but argued that if a person decided they wanted to die they had the right to kill themselves. Do you agree with this view? Do you think the magazine was right to publish the article?

CONSIDER

Objective

● To understand the reasons why divorce happens and to examine the rights children and young people have when parents divorce.

When a marriage breaks down

1. There was a time when it was almost unheard of for couples to divorce but the law in the UK now allows a couple to divorce if they can show that there has been an 'irretrievable breakdown' of the marriage. What does this phrase mean?

CONSIDER

2. The list below shows what the courts consider to be evidence of the breakdown of a marriage. Do you think these are reasonable grounds for divorce? Would you add any others?

> ● If one partner has committed adultery.
> ● If one partner has treated the other unreasonably, either by physical or mental cruelty, or insanity.
> ● If one partner has deserted the other for a continuous period of two years.
> ● If the couple have lived apart for two years and both consent to the divorce.
> ● If the partners have lived apart for five years but only one partner wishes to be divorced.

DISCUSS

3. The law gives clear reasons, but they sound rather impersonal. Actual couples may have many reasons for wishing to divorce. In pairs, discuss what kind of things might make a person want a divorce. Are there some problems that could be worked through so that the marriage could survive?

FACT TO THINK ABOUT ... FACT TO THINK ABOUT ... FACT TO THINK ABOUT ...

The current divorce rate in Britain is just over one in three. Predictions suggest that it may be one in two within the next ten years.

KEY WORDS   divorce judge   irretrievable breakdown   custody

4. Life can be very difficult for children whose parents are going through a divorce. Sometimes, a child may feel relief if the situation at home has been unbearable but, in most cases, there will be mixed feelings. List the problems children might face when their parents split up.

5. When a court makes a decision about where a child should live after a divorce, the welfare of the child is always the most important thing considered. The child's opinion will be taken into account, according to their age and understanding of the situation. Unless there is a good reason why the child should not see one parent, the court will try to see that the child has regular contact with both parents. Brainstorm the things that should be taken into account when deciding which parent a child should live with. Which of these things are most important?

BRAINSTORM

6. Design a leaflet or website for children whose parents are going through a divorce, giving advice on the problems they may be facing and how to cope with them. You should carry out research to find organisations that could help and include details of these.

7. In groups of three or four, role-play a court hearing where a mother and father, who are divorcing, each ask for custody of their child. The other person or people in the group should judge which parent should be given custody.

ROLE–PLAY

8. In the vast majority of cases, children are placed in the custody of the mother after a couple split up. What do you think are the reasons for this? Do you think this situation is right?

CONSIDER

25

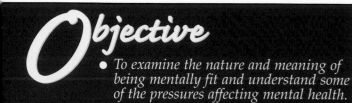

Mental health

Objective

- *To examine the nature and meaning of being mentally fit and understand some of the pressures affecting mental health.*

CONSIDER

1. Most people can describe what being physically fit means, but what does it mean to be mentally fit and healthy?

2. Mental illness still carries a stigma with it, but the fact is that the majority of people will suffer from mental health problems at some time in their lives. Depression, stress disorders, anxiety, phobias, addictions, eating disorders and many other conditions may all be mental health problems. Depression is a common mental health problem. People often say they are 'depressed' when they mean they are feeling sad or a bit low, but true depression is something that lasts for more than a short while and feels like it cannot be shaken off. Ffyona is suffering from depression. What signs might her friends notice that could suggest what she was suffering from?

Ffyona feels sad and empty. She cannot be bothered to do anything, she has no energy and her life seems pointless. She feels tired, yet she often cannot sleep, or wakes very early in the morning. She does not want to go out, see her friends, work or talk to people. Her thoughts tend to be negative – 'I'm ugly', 'I'm going to fail my exams', 'I'll never get a boyfriend', 'I'm no good at anything', 'No one really likes me'.

FACT TO THINK ABOUT ... FACT TO THINK ABOUT ... FACT TO THINK ABOUT ...

The number of young men attempting to harm themselves has doubled in the last ten years.

KEY WORDS   mental health   depression   suicide   self-harm

3. Ffyona's therapist has given her five minutes to draw a picture symbolising how she feels. Imagine that you are Ffyona and draw the picture. In pairs, discuss your drawings and what they show. Why do therapists sometimes use this technique to help people explore their problems?

DISCUSS

4. Depression, like many mental health problems, may have a physical cause. Research has found that people suffering from depression lack certain chemicals in the brain. Medicines can often help lift the person out of the depression, although they can take several weeks before they begin to work. Experts also believe that talking and sorting out problems is an important part of dealing with depression. Make a list of people who could help Ffyona. What could each of these people do?

CONSIDER

5. The Samaritans report that three young people harm themselves or attempt suicide in Britain every hour. What things might make a young person wish to harm themselves? What could you do if you felt like this? What could you do if you knew someone who felt like this?

6. You probably know what things you should and should not do to keep physically healthy. Brainstorm things you should and should not do in order to have the best chance of keeping mentally healthy. Now design a leaflet on mental health explaining what it means and the things you can do to help keep mentally healthy.

BRAINSTORM

Objective

● To examine the issue of violence in the home and explore strategies for dealing with it.

Violence in the home

1. 'Domestic violence' is the term used to describe violence between people living together. Experts think there could be as many as 35 000 cases of domestic violence each month in the United Kingdom. Of these, only around 20 per cent are reported to the police. Read the account by Aaron below.

> I can't remember a time when my dad didn't hit my mum. The first actual occasion I can remember I was about four. Dad came home and started shouting at Mum, then he got hold of her hair and started hitting her about the head. I was clinging on to his legs, trying to drag him off. I think there was a big fight about once a month.

> Now I'm 12 and we live in a flat. I've changed schools four times, and I used to get into trouble a lot. I used to fight. One day my mum said,"You're just like your dad," then we all cried and she said sorry. I don't see my dad anymore. I don't want to be like him.

> When she came out she seemed different. Someone had talked to her. One day, soon afterwards, I came downstairs and saw that Mum had packed some cases. A taxi came. I was about ten and my sister was about seven. We drove to a special refuge for women. We were there for a few months, then we were in a bed and breakfast for a bit but we still used to visit the refuge to talk to the people there and play in the playroom.

> In between times, Dad would just be out a lot. He used to push me out of the way but I don't remember him ever hitting me like he hit my mum. She left him once but then we went back again. I don't know why. One day I came home from school and Mum had been taken to hospital.

CONSIDER

2. Aaron was never hit by his father, but he was still a victim of domestic violence. How do you think life with his father affected Aaron? Do you think it will have any long-term effects?

3. One survey of women victims of domestic violence found that, on average, they received 35 beatings before they tried to get away from the relationship. Why do you think some victims of domestic violence find it hard to break away? Think about the practical things that might stop them from leaving as well as emotional things.

In 90 per cent of incidences of adult domestic violence, children are in the same or next room.

KEY WORDS | domestic violence   refuge   victim   abuse

4. People have strong views on domestic violence. Read the comments below. Do you agree or disagree? Discuss your opinions.

DISCUSS

> Many people who are violent came from violent homes themselves, but that does not mean that all victims of violence will become violent.

> Men often become violent when their partners make them angry so, in a way, some women deserve it.

> If you are violent towards a partner the responsibility is entirely yours – it doesn't matter what your background is or what the circumstances are – there are no excuses for it.

> Men can be victims of domestic violence too.

5. Many children who are victims of domestic violence, or who see it happening, are frightened to tell anyone. List the reasons a young person might give for not speaking to someone about domestic violence. Then design a poster encouraging young people in this situation to speak to someone.

Objective
- To examine child abuse within the family and to look at the rights of children within this context.

Problems in the family

1. The statement below guides all the work of The National Society for the Prevention of Cruelty to Children (NSPCC). What does it mean? How far off achieving this vision are we? What evidence shows that our society does not yet reach this standard?

> Our vision is a society where all children are loved, valued and able to fulfil their potential.

2. Abuse can come in many forms. Look at the stories below. In pairs, discuss what you could do if you, or someone you knew, was faced with a problem like one of these.

a. Gilly's mother is suffering from depression and cannot cope with her responsibilities as a mother. Gilly's mother locks her daughter in the bedroom for most of the day and puts the radio on loud so she cannot hear Gilly screaming.

b. Mick is 12. Ever since he can remember, his mum and dad have hit him. He has been hit repeatedly with hands, wooden spoons, belts, sticks, hairbrushes and other objects.

c. Elaine has been sexually abused by her uncle for the last three years. He has threatened that if she ever tells he will kill her and her mother.

d. Everyone who meets Moshan's family thinks they are all very happy but Moshan is desperately unhappy. Everything Moshan does is criticised by both his parents, who tell him he will never be any good at anything because he is so stupid.

FACT TO THINK ABOUT ... FACT TO THINK ABOUT ... FACT TO THINK ABOUT ...

Each week, at least one child in the UK dies, following abuse and neglect.

KEY WORDS abuse   protection   sexual abuse   incest

3. The NSPCC believes that most cruelty to children could be prevented. The box below shows some things that may be a factor in cases of child abuse. Copy and complete the table, making use of these factors. Add three other factors you think are relevant or important.

> poor education   adults' experiences as children
> drugs and alcohol   society's attitudes towards families   poverty

Factor	How might this contribute to child abuse?	What could be done to help?	Who could take this action?
Society's attitudes towards families	People don't like to interfere in another family's affairs. Society expects people to know how to be parents. Parents are expected to be able to control their children and those who can't cope may prefer to cover up what is happening rather than seek help, for fear of being labelled as 'bad parents'.	Publicity campaigns could point out that children are everyone's responsibility and encourage people to speak up if they think there is a problem. Better education could be provided about families, how they work and how to deal with problems.	The Government and charities such as the NSPCC. Schools could also teach about citizenship and people's responsibilities to one another. Schools could include more education on family life. Health visitors and family centres could run workshops.

4. Although there may be factors that make child abuse more likely, the responsibility for it lies with the person doing the abuse. Every child has the right to live without fear of abuse. Design a poster to encourage either victims of child abuse to seek help or adults who are abusing children to seek help. In each case, you will need to find out about organisations where these people could go to for help.

5. Many families can be supported so that child abuse stops and the family can stay together but, in some cases, the child is better off away from the family. In what situations do you think a child would be better off living with a foster family or in a residential home? Write down your answers.

CONSIDER

31

Objective

● To understand the feelings and emotions that may arise when a new family member arrives.

A new member of the family

CONSIDER

1. What circumstances can lead to a new member of the family arriving?

2. Change is often difficult, and changes within the family can be the most difficult to cope with because, for most people, the family is the place where they need to feel secure in order to cope with the rest of life. Look at the families below. For each person, write down two or three emotions that they might be feeling about the new situation. What problems might there be? What might help everyone adjust to the new situation?

a. When Sandra and Jim married, Sandra's son, Brannon, came to live with them and Jim's children, Louise and Christina, came to stay every weekend. After a difficult start, the family settled down into their new routines. Now, two years later, baby Chloe has arrived.

b. Karen and Phil married six years ago and Karen's children, Andrew and Neil, came to live with them. The whole family were delighted when Courtney was born and the boys love having a baby sister. Karen's mother, Peggy, moved in with them two years ago, and the family has got used to the changes this has involved. Now Phil's son, Darren, is moving in. Darren was living with his mother, but he is not getting on with his new stepfather and Phil wants to look after him. Phil has visited him regularly since leaving his mother, but the rest of the family have only met him twice because he lives several hundred miles away.

FACT TO THINK ABOUT ... FACT TO THINK ABOUT ... FACT TO THINK ABOUT ...

In one school where a survey was carried out, over a third of pupils could clearly remember a new member of the family arriving.

KEY WORDS   family   emotions   change   compromise   adjustment

IMAGINE

3. Imagine you are one of the characters (but not Chloe or Courtney) from the situations on page 32. Write three diary entries: one on the day you hear that the family is to have a new arrival, one on the day of the new arrival, and one several months later. Your diary should show how you feel as well as what happens.

DISCUSS

4. Talk about the problems below. What could each person do to try to improve the situation? What advice would you give each person?

> My new stepmum is very nice and she's trying really hard to get on with me, even though she's not that much older than I am! The trouble is, she can't cook. Everything is disgusting, but I don't want to upset her by telling her.

> My dad and I always used to have a cuddle watching telly but since my stepmum moved in she always sits next to him and I get left out.

> My dad's new girlfriend has really turned him against us. We used to get along fine but she always complains about us and he takes her side. I love my dad but she's stopping him from loving us.

> Everything my stepson does irritates me. The way he talks, the way he eats, the noise he makes. I just wish he'd move out again.

33

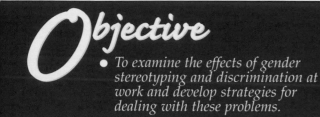

Objective

- To examine the effects of gender stereotyping and discrimination at work and develop strategies for dealing with these problems.

Problems at work

CONSIDER

1. Since the 1972 Sex Discrimination Act, the law states that all jobs, training and education (with a few exceptions) should be equally available to both men and women. Men and women should also be paid the same if they do the same job. Although things have changed, there are still many cases where men and women face discrimination. Look at each of the cases below and talk about the problems faced by the people involved. What attitudes and beliefs caused the problems? How could the issues have been tackled?

I applied for a Beauty Therapy course. The college said I could do Hairdressing but not Beauty Therapy because they said, "Women would not want a male dealing with very intimate areas of their body, for example when waxing bikini lines." I pointed out that there are male physios, doctors and nurses but they wouldn't listen. After a two-year battle, I was finally accepted on a Beauty Therapy course at another college.

I started work in an all-male office. I soon noticed that it was always me who was asked to make the tea, even though there were other people available to do it. Then the boss started making comments, at first about how I looked and what I wore, and then about my body and other sexual comments. When I complained, he said, "You're a woman in a male environment – you'll have to get used to it." After six months, I resigned and the Equal Opportunities Commission helped me take my boss to court. He was fined and lost his job.

On average, women earn less than men; when the average hourly earnings for men was £9.57 it was just £7.79 for women.

KEY WORDS   gender   stereotyping   discrimination   sexism

I trained as a mechanic and came top of my year in the practical assessments and second in the theory. I applied for a number of jobs but didn't get any interviews. Eventually, I filled out an application form without making it clear that I was female; I just signed it with my initial and surname. I was given an interview but when I turned up they said that office interviews had been the day before. When they found out I was there for the mechanic's job the boss told me it would be difficult for me to fit in and that they didn't have facilities for women. I eventually found a job elsewhere. The other mechanics are all male but we all get on really well and I've had no problems here.

I was a 'house-husband' for 15 years and have brought up four children. I've helped out at playgroup and school. I'm good with children and I'm good at art, cooking and other practical things. I applied for a teaching assistant post at a primary school where they didn't know me but I was told that, as the job was with very young children, they were really looking for a woman who would have 'the woman's touch and be caring towards the children'.

ROLE–PLAY

2. Most interviewers know that they are not supposed to discriminate because of gender, but they may find it hard to be fair in practice. Discrimination may come in the form of asking different questions, such as asking a woman, rather than a man, if she thinks she is strong enough for the job. In groups, role-play an interview where someone goes for a job that is traditionally thought of as unsuitable for their gender. Show your role-plays and discuss the issues raised.

3. Produce an advice sheet for pupils wanting to take up careers where they might encounter gender discrimination. Your leaflet should include information about laws and organisations that might be helpful.

Objective
● To understand the role and importance of modern technology in the workplace.

CONSIDER

1. The introduction of modern technology has changed many jobs almost beyond recognition. Read the comments below. What might the third comment be?

> I take notes using shorthand from my boss. Then I have to type up the letters and things. This morning I am typing 20 letters, inviting clients to a Christmas event. It's boring because they are all the same and if I make a mistake I have to type that letter again.

> I've just emailed 150 of our top customers, drawing their attention to a special offer we have at the moment. That took me about ten minutes. My boss has just phoned on his mobile to ask me to scan in an image of one of our products and send it via email to another client who's interested in it.

What will a secretary in the year 2051 be doing?

2. Everyone needs to be able to use technology in some form, even if it's only using a cashpoint machine or an automated petrol pump. Most jobs use technology too. The pictures below show one item of technology needed in that particular job. For each job, name two more.

It has been predicted that on-line shopping will become commonplace within 20 years and that shops, as we know them, will eventually become obsolete.

KEY WORDS   technology   workplace   'Brave New World'

3. Can you think of any job that doesn't use modern technology in any way?

4. Draw a picture of yourself in ten years time, carrying out a job you would like to do. In your picture, show all the different types of technology you will need to use in that job. (Remember – in ten years time, the technology may be different from what is used today.)

5. Nadim has begun to write two lists showing some of the things he can already do using modern technology, and some of the things he would like to learn. Write your own lists like Nadim's, showing what you can do and what you need to learn.

TECHNOLOGY

Things I can do:
send and read emails, surf the Internet, use a cashpoint, word process a letter, use a database.

Things I need to learn:
set up a database, install games and other software, open an on-line bank account.

6. What are the advantages of modern technology? Are there any disadvantages?

Objective
● To understand the nature of community-based voluntary groups, and explore their benefits for individuals and communities.

Community-based voluntary groups

ROLE-PLAY

1. Get together in a small group of about four or five.

Stapley is a small village of 800 people. Over the last 18 months, the village has been transformed from a group of loosely connected individuals to a tight-knit community where everyone feels involved. This has come about as a result of a community project that started in a small way and grew. Imagine you are a group of young people in Stapley. Make a video diary charting the progress of the community project outlined below. Your diary should feature different times in the project, and should show how the project has affected the lives of individuals and the community as a whole. You will need to role-play events and carry out interviews.

FACT TO THINK ABOUT ... FACT TO THINK ABOUT ... FACT TO THINK ABOUT ...

One Oxfordshire village of about 5000 people has more than 30 community-based voluntary groups.

KEY WORDS voluntary community benefits

My thanks go to everyone involved, from Farmer Dawson, who sold us the field at the nominal price and lent us his digger in the early stages, to the fundraisers, the people who cleared, planted and laid, volunteers who provided snacks and drinks every weekend, villagers who donated plants, people who babysat so that others could come and work here. In fact, I'd like to thank just about everyone in the village because this has been a true community project, and I know you will all agree with me when I say that not only did Stapley get a park and playground but it now has a thriving community spirit.

2. A book has been published on the Stapley park and playground project, featuring photographs and interviews with the people involved. Write the introduction to the book, outlining why the project was so important and what the benefits were.

3. There are all kinds of community-based voluntary groups, from ones like this to groups who will shop for the elderly, run summer play schemes, sports groups, youth clubs, PTAs, provide support and counselling, and all manner of other things. What kind of voluntary work do you think you would be good at? In what ways might you benefit from doing voluntary work?

CONSIDER

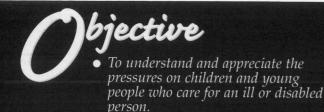

Objective

● To understand and appreciate the pressures on children and young people who care for an ill or disabled person.

Young carers

DISCUSS

1. Discuss the comments below. What are the problems with each viewpoint? Who do you think should care for ill or disabled people?

If someone needs long-term care then social services and the health authority should provide the resources. Nurses and cleaners could call in and meals should be delivered. It shouldn't be left to the families.

Yes, but there's no money for that sort of care and some people don't like to be looked after by strangers. Families should rally round and support each other. Friends and neighbours should help too.

Rubbish. Someone who needs a lot of care should be in a hospital or a home. You shouldn't be allowed to choose to stay at home if it's going to wreck your family's lives.

2. Whatever you think about how disabled and ill people should be looked after, the fact is that hundreds of thousands of people are looked after in their own homes, mostly by relatives. A significant number of these are cared for by young people. Read the story below.

Russell is 16. He lives with his 13-year-old sister and his mother, who has rheumatoid arthritis. For the last three years, his mother has been very disabled. Russell does all the cooking and most of the cleaning. He helps his mother dress, helps her in and out of the bath, empties her commode, and does the shopping. Russell's sister, Tracey, does all the washing and some of the cleaning. When Russell's mother is particularly bad he stays home from school. The family have never told anyone how much Russell and Tracey have to do because they are afraid that they will be taken into care. Russell says, "I've failed all my exams and I won't be able to work because I have to take time off to look after Mum, but it's better than seeing the family split up."

Around 50 000 young people in the United Kingdom are providing regular or substantial care to an ill or disabled parent.

KEY WORDS   carer   support   ill   disabled

ROLE–PLAY

3. Recently, Russell has started writing to a girl he met on the Internet. He has decided to be honest with her. Write a letter from Russell in which he tells his new friend about the lifestyle he leads and how he feels about it. When you have finished, swap letters with a partner and write replies to each other's letters from the friend.

CONSIDER

4. It is estimated that every school in the country has at least one pupil who is providing care for a relative at home. What could schools do to help these pupils? What could their friends do?

5. There are some projects that aim to help young carers. These are clubs where carers can meet up to talk about their problems, or play games and forget them for a while. There are different opinions about this kind of support. Read the opinions below. What do you think?

> These clubs are a cheap way of pretending society is helping. Young people shouldn't be doing this level of caring anyway. We should invest more money in social services and the health service to make sure that young people don't have to care for relatives like this.

> It's easy to say they shouldn't be caring for their relatives but the fact is that thousands do and they need support. There will never be enough money to prevent the problem. Support clubs are a good idea. They help the youngsters see that they are not alone and give them a chance to have a break with others who understand them.

Regional government

1. In 1997 and 1998, the people of Scotland, Wales and Northern Ireland voted in favour of devolved government. As a result, the Welsh Assembly, the Northern Ireland Assembly and the Scottish Parliament were set up to take over some of the government of those regions. Read the comments below and list the reasons people voted for devolved government.

> In Wales, we have our own culture and way of life. We have our own language. The Welsh Assembly will put Welsh people first. For example, UK Government policy hasn't always helped Welsh farming and industry. The Assembly will be a real voice for Wales and will answer to the Welsh people.

> Many Scots feel Scottish, not British. Like some Welsh and Irish people, there are some Scots who would like to be completely independent of England. The Scottish Parliament is a step in the right direction. It isn't right for one country to have complete control over another.

> Northern Ireland desperately needs peace. A Northern Ireland Assembly will give people the chance to have their say in how the country is run.

FACT TO THINK ABOUT ... FACT TO THINK ABOUT ... FACT TO THINK ABOUT ...

Of the three regional governments, only the Scottish Parliament is able to raise or reduce tax levels.

KEY WORDS | devolution   regional government   regional assembly

CONSIDER

2. Some powers stay with the UK Government but many decisions are now made at a regional level. Look at the two boxes below. Why has the Government in London decided to keep the powers in the left-hand box? If you lived in one of the regions, how could your life be affected by decisions made at a regional level? Write down three examples of things that a regional government might decide that could affect you if you lived in that region.

> The UK Government will control foreign policy, defence and security, decisions about the money system, employment laws, social security laws and transport safety.

> Regional governments or assemblies will be able to make decisions about health care, education, housing, local development, transport systems, the environment, agriculture, sports and arts.

3. What are the advantages of devolved government? Are there any disadvantages?

DISCUSS

4. The UK Government still includes MPs from Wales, Scotland and Northern Ireland as well as England. This means that MPs from those areas can vote on issues affecting England, but MPs from English constituencies cannot vote on issues decided at a regional level. Working in a small group, decide whether or not you think England should have its own regional parliament. Share your opinions as a class giving reasons for your decisions.

5. The person below is against the whole idea of regional governments. Write a reply to this man saying whether or not you agree with his views and giving your reasons.

> There was a time when people were proud to be part of the United Kingdom. Now it seems parts of it are trying to break away. It's ridiculous to have four different governing bodies in one country. We've got one monarch, a united flag and a common language. We should be ruled by one government.

Running away

Objective
● *To gain an understanding of the reasons why some young people run away from home and to examine the dangers they face.*

BRAINSTORM

1. Brainstorm reasons why a young person might decide to run away from home. Keep the list safe to use later in the lesson.

2. The script below is about two 15-year-olds, Neil and Meera, who have both run away from their homes and have been sleeping on the streets. Meera has found an old coat. She is sitting on a park bench with the coat beside her when Neil sees it. He thinks the coat has been dumped and tries to take it. In pairs, read the script.

Meera:	Hey, that's mine.
Neil:	Sorry. I thought it had been dumped and I'm a bit cold.
Meera:	You look terrible. Have you been sleeping rough?
Neil:	Yeah. About two weeks. What about you?
Meera:	Me too. I nicked this coat from a bloke on the tube. What are you doing for food?
Neil:	Going hungry mostly. I've been taking stuff from a supermarket but last time I nearly got caught. Then I tried begging but I only got 75p. I'm thinking about going back home.
Meera:	Why did you leave?
Neil:	I couldn't stand it. My mum's boyfriend moved in. He's all right some of the time but he drinks a lot. When he's drunk he shouts and throws stuff. He pushed Mum about and then he started on me. Mum says he's got a lot of problems and that I should be more understanding. She can't see he's just like my dad used to be. My dad half-killed both of us before she left him. I'm not going through that again.
Meera:	So why go back home?
Neil:	Anything's better than this. Maybe I could talk to someone. I don't know. Mum will be worried though. Besides, I've got no money.
Meera:	I'm not going home. My dad does more than just push me about. I'm not saying any more. Look. I'm supposed to be meeting a man here tonight who said he'd find work for me. Why don't you stay too?
Neil:	Are you crazy? You're too young to get a proper job so it will either be drug dealing or prostitution! Why don't you go home and tell someone what's happening?
Meera:	No thanks. I'd rather take my chances here. The man I'm meeting seemed really nice. He bought me a meal and really seemed to care about me.
Neil:	You're mad. Do you know how most runaways end up?
Meera:	Well, it's my life.
Neil:	Well I just hope it's a life worth living.

FACT TO THINK ABOUT ... FACT TO THINK ABOUT ... FACT TO THINK ABOUT ...

One third of runaways run to escape from some kind of abuse.

KEY WORDS   hostel   squat   sleeping rough   abuse   prostitution

CONSIDER

3. Talk about what has happened to Neil and Meera and what they have decided to do. What might happen to Meera? If she really feels she cannot go home, what else could she do, rather than meeting with this man?

4. Write or perform a play script about a young person who runs away from home. Your play should show why they ran away, how they tried to survive on the streets, and what happened to them.

5. Look back at the list you made at the beginning of the lesson, showing reasons why young people run away from home. For each one, suggest something that a young person faced with that problem could do apart from running away.

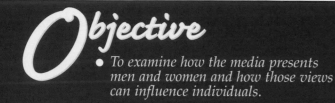
According to the media

CONSIDER

1. Look at the activities listed in the box below. On television, which of the activities are most often done by women, and which are most often done by men? Try to think of recent examples that you have seen. When men and women are shown doing these things, is there any difference in how they are seen to be doing them?

Running a business.
Telling others what to do.
Falling over.
Doing practical things.
Selling cars in an advert.
Cleaning up.
Looking after a family.
Working in an office.

● Partly clothed.
● Asking for advice on looks.
● Causing problems in relationships.
● Looking good.
● Shopping.

2. Now think about pictures in newspapers and magazines. Are men or women shown most often in the ways listed? Again, talk about any differences between the way men and women are shown in these situations.

3. Thinking about the things you have discussed so far this lesson, describe, in a few sentences, how you think men are portrayed by the media and how you think women are portrayed by the media. Does the media simply portray the way women and men really are in our society or is it lagging behind changes that are taking place? Does it influence the way men and women are treated in real life?

A recent survey found that when practical jobs (such as farming, engineering and driving) were shown in films, soaps and other programmes on television, the person carrying out the job was male in 87 per cent of cases.

KEY WORDS   media   stereotype   sexism   portrayal

CONSIDER

4. Some newspapers today are more cautious about making very sexist comments, but cartoons can often get away with more. Do you find the cartoons below funny? What values or beliefs do they seem to be upholding? Do they represent some people's opinions or are they out of date now? Would they influence how people feel about the events being commented on? Why do cartoons like this still appear in newspapers?

This cartoon follows an occasion when a footballer was seen crying after being sent off during a match.

This cartoon followed an appeal by a large union for more women to enter the building trades.

5. Working in a group, produce a newspaper page that challenges what you see as the current media messages about male and female roles. Your page should include realistic stories and you should think carefully about the pictures you choose to use.

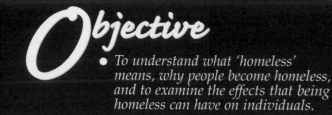

Groups in society – homeless people

CONSIDER

1. When you hear the words 'homeless person' what image comes to mind?

DISCUSS

2. The people below are all homeless. Read the information. Discuss why each person became homeless and how being homeless is affecting them.

When I told my parents I was a lesbian, Dad hit the roof and I decided to leave. Since then, I've been moving around staying with different friends and trying to get a job. I've had to leave college because I didn't have the money to get there from all the different places I've been staying. Friends have been very kind but I don't feel I can stay anywhere too long. I live out of a suitcase.

I spent years in and out of mental hospitals. The last time I was discharged, the social worker sorted out a flat for me but, after he stopped visiting, it all went wrong. I got depressed and chucked in my job, then my money ran out and I couldn't pay the rent. I ended up sleeping on the streets. I know I ought to see a doctor but it's difficult when you're homeless.

My husband used to hit me and one day I finally left him. I spent two months with my three young children in a women's refuge and now we're in temporary accommodation in a bed and breakfast. We have one room, a cold tap, a kettle and a little two-ring cooker. Kit has been to three different schools because of all the moves.

After I was made redundant, we couldn't afford the mortgage and our house was repossessed. My mother offered to put us up, but it's terrible because my wife, the baby and I are all in one room. My wife and mother don't get on either. My wife and baby have gone to stay with her parents for a few weeks but I've stayed here to try and get a job.

One social report claimed that 'A home is more than having a roof over your head. It is a place to be secure, where people can grow, have privacy and space.'

KEY WORDS   homeless   hostel   refuge   home

3. List what you regard as the essential features of a home for anyone.

4. The statistics below show local authority figures on homeless households in one year. A 'household' may be one person or may be a whole family. Write down what you understand by the phrases 'priority need', 'intentionally homeless' and 'not in priority need'.

CONSIDER

Region	North East	London
Number of homeless households	9160	41070
Estimated number of homeless individuals within these households	22000	98600
Number of homeless households in priority need	4890	27220
Number of homeless households found to be intentionally homeless	590	1470
Number of homeless households not in priority need	3680	12380

5. You are making a documentary about homelessness and have found a homeless family who have agreed to take part. Write or role-play interviews with various members of the family to find out how they became homeless, and how it is affecting each of them.

ROLE-PLAY

6. Carry out research to find out what organisations exist to help homeless people. Then design a poster giving advice to homeless people about the best place to find help.

RESEARCH

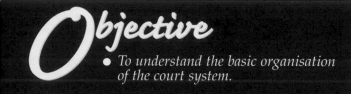
The court system

BRAINSTORM

1. Brainstorm reasons why people break the law. Which laws are commonly broken?

2. The law in the United Kingdom can be grouped under two headings. Read the information below.

a. Criminal law
This includes crimes against a person – such as assault, murder; crimes against property – such as theft, vandalism; traffic offences; sexual offences and crimes against the state, such as spying or smuggling.

b. Civil law
This concerns the private rights of people, such as disputes to do with contracts, buying and selling things, family and divorce matters.

CONSIDER

3. Which of the cases below would be tried under criminal law, and which are civil cases?

| Ms A was found guilty of driving at 50mph in a 30mph speed limit. | Mr B took his lodger to court for failing to pay the rent. | Mr C was accused of damaging his neighbour's house. |

4. Scotland has separate courts for civil and criminal cases. Minor offences are heard by a sheriff, who is usually a trained advocate or solicitor. More serious offences are heard by a sheriff or judge, and a jury. In other parts of the UK, 95 per cent of criminal cases are heard in a magistrates' court. This is a court where three or more magistrates hear the case. Witnesses can be called, but there is no jury. Read the information about magistrates on page 51. Design an advert asking people to consider being magistrates. Your advert should include a list of skills, qualities and experiences you think someone would need in order to be a good magistrate.

If someone who has been found guilty can show that the trial was unfair in some way, or that new evidence has come to light, they may appeal. If their appeal is accepted then the case will be heard again.

KEY WORDS   jury   magistrate   judge   court

Magistrates are volunteers. They are drawn from the local community, but tend to be well-educated people working in business or the service sector. They need have no previous legal training, although they do receive some training before taking up their duties. They have limited sentencing powers, but can give prison sentences of up to one year.

5. More serious criminal cases are referred to the Crown Court, where the case is heard in front of a jury. A jury consists of 12 people between the ages of 18 and 70 who have been called for jury service. These are ordinary men and women on the register of electors. It is the jury, not the judge, who decides whether the defendant (person being tried) is guilty or not guilty. The judge decides on the sentence to impose if the person is found guilty.

   Read the opinion below. List the advantages and disadvantages of the jury system, then hold a debate using the opinion below as a starting point.

The jury system is expensive, time consuming and unreliable. We shouldn't rely on amateurs to make important decisions.

6. County courts can only deal with civil cases. Cases are heard by registrars or judges who are trained and experienced lawyers. Most divorce cases are held in county courts. They also hear cases regarding contracts, adoption, claims for damages, cases to do with racial and sexual discrimination and many other civil cases. Why do you think some cases need to be judged by trained lawyers rather than volunteer magistrates?

CONSIDER

7. Make a list of all the words associated with courts and the law on this page, and any others you know of. Use these to compile a glossary of legal terms that could be included in a young person's guide to the law.

Juvenile court

1. Juvenile courts hear cases concerning young people under 17. Three magistrates hear the case. Read the comments below to find out more about juvenile courts.

> I am a magistrate with special training to hear young people's cases. We try to make the court case informal. We wear normal clothes, have tables and chairs instead of benches and try to explain things clearly.

> I went with my son to the juvenile court because he had to have a parent with him. We sat at the front, facing the magistrates with our lawyer next to us. They did explain things but I didn't always understand what they said.

> The juvenile court was smaller than I expected. The press were there but the judge ruled that they couldn't print my name. My social worker was there too. We waited two weeks before going back for the sentence so that the magistrates could read the reports on me.

2. Using the information above, produce a chart showing some of the features of a juvenile court and explaining how these features might be helpful to young people appearing in court. The chart below will get you started.

Features of the court	How this might help young people
Magistrates are specially trained to deal with young people	This would make them better at understanding and talking to children

FACTS TO THINK ABOUT ... FACTS TO THINK ABOUT ... FACTS TO THINK ABOUT ..

Between the ages of ten and fourteen, a child can be prosecuted for an offence, but the prosecuting lawyers have to show that the child knew they were doing wrong. After the age of fourteen, it is assumed the young person knows right from wrong.

KEY WORDS   magistrate   juvenile   criminal offence   sentence   lawyer

CONSIDER

3. Look at the offences given below. What sentence do you think should be imposed in each case? Be prepared to explain your decision.
   - A 12-year-old boy caught shoplifting for the first time.
   - A 15-year-old girl found breaking into a house and stealing video tapes and computer games. She already had a conditional discharge for shoplifting.
   - A 14-year-old boy who keeps breaking into cars and driving them. His parents feel they cannot control him.
   - A 16-year-old girl who gave an ecstasy tablet to a friend.

4. Young people who commit serious crimes, or who keep breaking the law, can face serious consequences. Why do you think the judges imposed the following orders?:

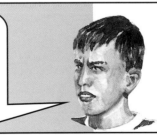

I was always in trouble with the police. In the end, I was taken into care. The local authority decide where I live. I was in a home for a while but since I've kept out of trouble they've let me live with my dad again.

I kept getting into fights at football matches. I was placed under an attendance order, which means I have to attend a special centre. I have to go on Saturday afternoons. We talk a bit, then work out in the gym. I wouldn't mind but I miss the matches.

I was sent to a detention centre for a month - boys aged 14 to 21 can be sent there. It was terrible - like a cross between prison and the army. Now I see a probation officer each week.

I was sent to prison. They call it 'youth custody' but it was in part of the adult prison and I couldn't see any difference except we had to do school work.

5. Write a letter from a young person to a friend who has been in trouble with the police, saying what they did, what happened to them and how they felt about it.

Objective
● To examine the work of a local councillor in order to understand the way in which councils work.

The work of a local councillor

1. Local councillors are not paid for the work they do, although they may claim expenses. Brainstorm the reasons why someone might want to be a local councillor.

2. Dave has been a councillor for four years and is about to stand for election again. What work does Dave do in the council? How does he spend most of his time? What do the local people think of him?

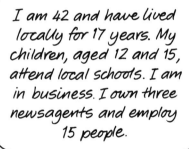

> I am 42 and have lived locally for 17 years. My children, aged 12 and 15, attend local schools. I am in business. I own three newsagents and employ 15 people.

> Dave has been interested in making communities work all the time we've been married. I sometimes get fed up with the endless phone calls we get, but I'm proud of the things he has achieved, like helping to get a road crossing outside the school.

> Dave is brilliant. He listens and tries to help. We talked to him about the problems of kids having nowhere to go and he suggested we start a club. He even helps out twice a week and has persuaded several businesses to donate games and equipment.

> Dave is honest and caring. We spoke to him about the litter from the local takeaway and he got involved to sort it out. He's what we need on the council – somebody who gets his finger out and makes people listen.

FACT TO THINK ABOUT ... FACT TO THINK ABOUT ... FACT TO THINK ABOUT ...

Many local councillors are self-employed or retired.

KEY WORDS   councillor   ward   committee   expenses

3. Using the information from this page, put together an election leaflet telling people about Dave and explaining why they should vote for him.

Concerns raised at this month's two-ward surgeries
Cars driven too fast through estate.
Young people hanging around shops and causing a problem.
Dog dirt in children's play area.
Lorries from local quarry causing dirt and dust. Proposed closure of primary school.
Dumping of rubbish at St John's Wood.

Monday   2pm Ward surgery
            6pm Youth group
Tuesday   3pm Finance committee meeting
            7pm Full council meeting
Wednesday
Thursday   7.30pm AGM at day care centre
Friday   1pm Meet with Jon to visit woods re rubbish problem
            6pm Youth group
Saturday   12 noon Meet with tennis club chair to discuss lottery bid for floodlights
Sunday   Barbara and Jeff for lunch

The following list shows which committees each councillor stands on.

| Dave Linch | Finance, Social Services, Parks and Cemeteries (vice chair) |

CONSIDER

4. One of the problems Dave is concerned with at the moment is that people are dumping rubbish in some woodland, which is a local beauty spot. He has arranged to visit the woodland with another councillor to see the problem for himself. What action could Dave and the local council take to solve this problem?

PLAN

5. Some councils are trying to attract more people from ethnic minorities to stand as local councillors. Plan a radio appeal asking for people, particularly those from ethnic minorities, to consider being councillors. What will you say to convince someone that being a councillor is worthwhile?

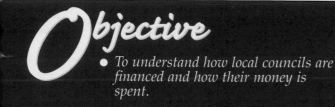

Finances and local government

CONSIDER

1. Which of the following services are provided by local government?

- ● Education
- ● Libraries
- ● Social services
- ● Police
- ● Fire service
- ● Waste management
- ● Trading standards

2. Local government receives money from the UK Government and from local council tax, which is paid by every household. The figures on page 57 show how one council spent its income of £1 110 million on the services it provides in one year. For each of the services listed, give an example of something the money might be spent on. For example, community safety might include money for road crossing patrols.

3. Using the information from the chart on page 57, produce a pie chart showing how the money was spent. What is the largest expense for this council?

FACT TO THINK ABOUT ... FACT TO THINK ABOUT ... FACT TO THINK ABOUT ...

All council finances are 'audited'. This means they are checked carefully by outside agencies to make sure that the council is being honest and accurate.

KEY WORDS	council tax expenditure revenue

Service	Amount spent in £ millions
Education	644.5
Libraries and information	20.5
Heritage and culture	4.0
Social services	269.0
Highways and transportation	75.2
Waste management	20.5
Community safety	4.8
Planning	7.5
Enterprise	4.5
Fire service	37.0
Other services	22.5
TOTAL	**1110.0**

IMAGINE

4. Decisions about how to spend money are made by elected councillors. Working in a small group, imagine you are councillors. Several suggestions have been made about new projects that would benefit your area. As there is no extra money, any new project that goes ahead will have to be paid for by a cut in services elsewhere. Decide which of the new projects listed below should go ahead and, for each one, say which service cut will pay for it.

New projects
- open women's refuge for victims of domestic violence
- open two new youth centres on the largest estates
- computerise the libraries
- open a play centre to cater for disabled children and their parents
- build new recycling facilities at four areas in the town

Cuts in service
- increase class sizes by two pupils per class
- close mobile library service
- close two small museums
- reduce number of home helps for the elderly
- cut youth club staff by raising the youth club age from ten to thirteen

CONSIDER

5. Share your decisions as a class, giving reasons for your choices. How did you decide what to fund and what to cut?

6. Imagine that your local councillors have decided to close a day centre for the elderly. How could you persuade them to change their decision? What types of campaign are likely to be most successful?

Managing the country – finances

1. Match the words in the box to the correct definition below.

Budget
Chancellor of the Exchequer
Tax
Government revenue
Government expenditure

a. The money that the Government receives.
b. The Cabinet Minister responsible for Government finances.
c. What the Government spends.
d. An annual statement detailing the Government's spending plans for the forthcoming year.
e. Money paid to the Government from people, businesses or organisations.

2. The Government controls billions of pounds every year. List at least ten things that the Government pays for.

3. The Government's income comes from taxes. Some of this money is invested in order to generate more money, the rest is spent. Look at the way in which Seema pays tax to the Government.

Gross pay	£1123.25
Tax	£143.35
National Insurance	£90.16
Total deduction	£233.51
Net pay	£889.74

Seema can earn a certain amount of money without paying tax but, once she earns over a certain limit in any one year, she pays a percentage of the rest as tax to the Government. This is called 'direct tax' because it is paid directly to the Government's Inland Revenue department.

Seema pays road tax each year on her car.

National Insurance is a type of direct tax. People who work pay National Insurance contributions, and this money is used to provide state pensions to retired people, sickness benefit, and other benefits such as maternity pay.

Seema pays tax on the interest she earns from her savings. Her bank and building society work it out and pay it directly to the Inland Revenue for her. If she didn't earn enough to pay tax she could claim this back.

Most goods that Seema buys are taxed. VAT stands for 'value added tax'. This means that a certain percentage of the money goes to the Government. Some things, like tobacco and alcohol, carry very high levels of tax, so the Government receives a lot of money from the sale of these goods. Taxes on goods and services are called indirect taxes. They are collected by 'Customs and Excise'.

FACT TO THINK ABOUT ... FACT TO THINK ABOUT ... FACT TO THINK ABOUT ...

Since 1942, the Welfare State has looked after people 'from the cradle to the grave'.

KEY WORDS   finances   tax   Chancellor of the Exchequer

4. The Chancellor of the Exchequer is the person in charge of 'balancing the books' for the country. It is one of the most important jobs in the Government. Read the thoughts that are keeping this Chancellor awake.

> I'd like to spend billions of extra pounds on education and health, but this money has to come from somewhere. Will people be happy to pay more tax if they get better public services in return, or should I cut the tax rate, which might make us more popular so that we get elected again?

> I have to prepare the budget each year; the budget is a detailed account of how the Government will raise money and how it will spend it.

> Inflation is the rate at which prices go up. If I encourage pay rises by giving teachers, nurses and civil servants a big pay increase, people will have more money to spend, which might put inflation up.

> Did I remember to put the cat out?

5. Design a cartoon character who would appeal to young people and produce a cartoon page that will teach young people about Government finances.

6. Consider the question below and write two answers – one from a top executive who earns over a million pounds a year and one from an unemployed person. In each case, include reasons for that person's opinion.

CONSIDER

What do you think is fairer – tax on earnings or tax on goods and services?

Political parties

Objective

● To gain an understanding of the political party system in the United Kingdom.

1. Some Members of Parliament stand as 'independent' candidates. This means they are not members of a political party. The majority of MPs, however, do belong to political parties. Read the information to find out what we mean by a political party.

● A political party is an organisation that seeks to influence politics through campaigning and political representation (at national, regional and local levels).

● Party members hold broadly similar political views with others of the same party and, although there will be differences of opinion, they work together to reach agreements that can then be presented as the party position.

● Members usually pay a subscription fee that helps fund party work.

● Members do not have to be involved with the work of the party, but many help to organise campaigns, fund-raise and support elected representatives.

● Party members vote to choose the candidates who will stand for local and general elections.

CONSIDER

2. What would politics in this country be like if there were no party system and everyone was independent? What are the advantages of having a party system? What are the disadvantages?

FACT TO THINK ABOUT ... FACT TO THINK ABOUT ... FACT TO THINK ABOUT ...

Fewer than one million people are members of the three largest political parties.

KEY WORDS   political party   minor party   nationalist parties

RESEARCH

3. The information below tells you about some of the political parties working in the United Kingdom. Carry out research to find out more about some of these, or other, parties and produce fact files showing:
   ● who the party leader is
   ● how many seats in parliament it currently holds
   ● what its main policies are.

The Conservative Party	The Conservative Party emerged from the Tory Party in about 1834 when Robert Peel became leader. His aim was to develop a party that would represent the interests of all wealthy people, whether it was wealth from property, land, industry or other sources.
The Labour Party	The Labour Representative Committee was set up in 1900, and was renamed the Labour Party in 1906. It was set up to represent the interests of the working class people, who had not been entitled to vote in the previous century.
The Liberal Democrats	The Liberal Democrat Party came into being in 1988 when the Liberal Party merged with the Social Democrat Party (SDP). The SDP was formed in 1981 by a group of former Labour Party members. The Liberal Party was formed in 1859.
Plaid Cymru	Plaid Cymru was founded in 1925. One of its aims is an independent Wales.
The Scottish National Party	The SNP was founded in 1934 when two other parties merged. One of its aims is an independent Scotland.
The Ulster Unionist Party	This party governed Northern Ireland from the time when it was set up as a province in 1922 until direct rule was imposed in 1972. It is a Protestant party.

4. Design a page for an encyclopaedia or website about the United Kingdom party system for pupils a year or two younger than yourself. (You may want to find out about other political parties before you begin.) You could also design a second page about one particular party using the information you collected.

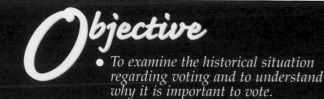

Why vote?

Objective
- To examine the historical situation regarding voting and to understand why it is important to vote.

Dear pupils,

From now on, only pupils over the age of 15 who are taking more than eight exam courses will be allowed to vote in school council elections. This is because the school council is very important and the rest of you are too young and too uneducated to be able to make sensible decisions about who should represent you.

Yours sincerely,
Your Headteacher

1. Read the letter. How would you feel if your headteacher sent this letter out in your school? What arguments would you use to try to change your headteacher's mind?

2. You probably can't imagine your headteacher sending out a letter like the one above but, in the nineteenth century, arguments like these were used to prevent most of the population in the UK from voting. It was argued that only men with a large amount of property had the education and experience to be allowed to vote. Look at the time line below, which shows the main steps in the battle to win the right to vote for all adults.

The only people who could vote were men who owned large amounts of property. This was about five per cent of the male population.	The First and Second Reform Acts and the Franchise Act each reduced the amount of property that entitled a man to vote. First, seven per cent of the male population could vote, then 16 per cent, then 28 per cent.	The Representation of the Peoples Act gave the vote to all men over the age of 21, and all women over the age of 30.

1800   1832   1867   1884   1918

The Equal Franchise Act gave women the right to vote at 21 – the same age as men.	The voting age for men and women was lowered to 18.

1928   1969

FACT TO THINK ABOUT … FACT TO THINK ABOUT … FACT TO THINK ABOUT …

On 4 June 1913, suffragette Emily Davison threw herself under the King's racehorse and was killed. She did this in order to raise awareness of the suffragette movement.

KEY WORDS | universal franchise vote suffragettes militancy

CONSIDER

3. Read the comments below. The woman on the right is about to explain why she thinks the other three people should use their votes. Write out what she might say. Make sure you answer each of the points made by the other three people.

> Voting doesn't make any difference – it doesn't change what the Government decides to do.

> With millions of people voting, what difference will my one vote make anyway?

> All the political parties are as bad as each other, so there's no point in voting.

> Just imagine if there wasn't a voting system. Voting is important because…

4. Women had a particularly hard time winning the vote. The campaign began peacefully but, by 1913, many suffragettes had become militant and the newspapers were full of accounts of women breaking windows, setting fire to buildings, chaining themselves to railings, planting bombs and going on hunger strike in prison. Imagine you were a suffragette in 1913. Write a letter either explaining why you have decided to use violent campaign methods or why you think it is wrong to use violent campaign methods.

COMPARE

5. In most democracies, people can choose whether or not to vote, but in a few countries (for example, Austria and Brazil) people have to vote. This is called 'compulsory voting'. List arguments for and against compulsory voting, then say whether or not you think voting should be compulsory or not and give your reasons.

6. You will have the right to vote when you are 18. What responsibilities will this right bring?

Objective

● *To explore the benefits of active involvement with school and local communities.*

Being involved

CONSIDER

1. Anna and Tan both get involved with the life of their school and communities. Look at the pictures below. Do you think their work makes a difference to people in their area? What do you think Anna and Tan get out of it?

a. Anna helped set up and run a school tuck shop.

b. Tan is chairperson of the school council.

c. Anna is part of a volunteer team organised by the youth club. Once a week, she spends an hour helping other people, such as gardening or shopping for the elderly, dog walking or helping at the community centre crèche.

d. Tan spends Saturday mornings working with a volunteer group that is trying to improve the area. So far, they have cleared a small stream, planted bulbs and repainted the playground equipment.

FACT TO THINK ABOUT ... FACT TO THINK ABOUT ... FACT TO THINK ABOUT ...

Research shows that planning and taking the initiative gives young people a great sense of self-worth.

KEY WORDS community   involvement   citizenship   initiative

e. Anna and Tan are both mentors in their school. This means that younger pupils can come to them with problems for advice and support.

2. Anna and Tan have just won the 'Young People Make a Difference' award. They are going to take part in a television programme about young people and have been given a list of the questions they are going to be asked. Write a script for the programme using the questions below and giving Anna and Tan's answers.

> **a.** Tell us about your involvement with the community. What sort of things do you do?
> **b.** This must take up a lot of your time. Why do you do it?
> **c.** Why should young people get involved in their communities? Why not leave it up to the adults?
> **d.** How do you feel about winning the award?

3. After leaving school, Anna and Tan will both apply for traineeships. Write a reference for either Anna or Tan from one of the adults who has worked with them on community projects. Your reference should mention their skills and achievements.

4. Put together a proposal for a community project for your area. It should be something that young people could get involved in. Your plan should include why there is a need for this project, who could be involved, how it will be funded and organised and how you will judge whether or not it is a success.

PLAN

5. Design a leaflet that could be given to 14 to 16 year olds with the title 'Being involved'. Your leaflet should encourage young people to get involved with their local communities and explain how the young people and the communities might both benefit.

Resolving world conflict

1. Begin by reading the information below.

> During the Second World War, Yugoslavia was taken over by Nazi Germany. Many Serbians were against the Nazis but many Croats supported the Nazis, and the two groups fought fiercely. Thousands died.

> After the war, Tito became president. The country was organised into six republics and although many groups still disliked each other, they managed to live together peacefully.

> There were many different cultures and many people never thought of themselves as Yugoslavs.

> In 1980 Tito died. Different groups wanted independence. Fighting began and some groups tried to wipe out others.

> The people belonged to different ethnic groups, including Serbs, Croats, Albanians, Turks and others.

> Yugoslavia was created after the First World War by joining several smaller countries.

> Some areas became independent countries quite peacefully but, in others, fighting continues.

2. It can be difficult to understand why people cannot reach agreement in the region. The people below each have an idea of how the problems in the area could be solved. Write the answer that Sofia might give to each suggestion.

> People should just forget their differences and learn to live together in peace.

Sofia was brought up in an area where Croats and Serbians lived together. When fighting began, her husband and brother were killed and she was forced to run away with her two children. She does not know if her parents or her sisters are alive. She wants to return home to the village she has lived in all her life but she is too afraid.

> We should threaten to bomb them if they don't stop fighting.

> There should be a vote and the group with the biggest vote should be allowed to rule.

> Each ethnic group should be given its own area and people should be made to move there. Then they could all live separately.

FACT TO THINK ABOUT ... FACT TO THINK ABOUT ... FACT TO THINK ABOUT ...

Over 1600 UN peacemakers have died whilst trying to keep the peace since 1948.

KEY WORDS United Nations   peacekeeping forces   ethnic group

CONSIDER

3. The United Nations aims to help restore peace in countries where conflict exists. The list below shows some of the things the UN has done to try to solve the conflict in the Yugoslavian region. For each action, list what the effects on Yugoslavia might have been. How could these have helped to end the fighting?

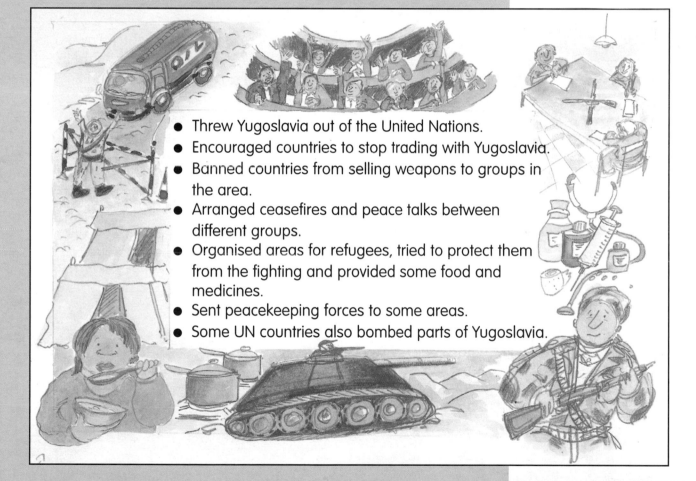

- Threw Yugoslavia out of the United Nations.
- Encouraged countries to stop trading with Yugoslavia.
- Banned countries from selling weapons to groups in the area.
- Arranged ceasefires and peace talks between different groups.
- Organised areas for refugees, tried to protect them from the fighting and provided some food and medicines.
- Sent peacekeeping forces to some areas.
- Some UN countries also bombed parts of Yugoslavia.

DISCUSS

4. Imagine that a problem similar to those of the Yugoslav region has broken out somewhere else in the world. You are part of a UN committee that has to decide how to respond. Discuss the actions you could take, then write a report describing three actions you will take and explaining how these will help restore peace in the area.

CONSIDER

5. Should countries be allowed to run themselves, or are there times when other countries should step in to deal with problems? What are the advantages of countries getting together to sort out problems? What are the disadvantages?

Objective
● To examine the implications of the world as an interdependent community in political and economic terms.

A global community – political and economic

BRAINSTORM

1. Countries have been trading with each other for thousands of years, but the scale of trading has changed. Where once it would have taken many months for a ship to travel from China carrying silks for Europe, today, transactions can take place through computer technology within seconds. What inventions have made world trade easier?

CONSIDER

2. In 1973, worldwide oil prices rose by 70 per cent, following the Yom Kippur War on Israel's borders. In 1987, a crash on the New York stock exchange affected trading around the world; thousands of investors lost huge amounts of money. In 2000, a surge for demand in oil and limited production resulted in a rapid rise in petrol prices. What do these three events tell you about world trade? Why does the price of oil have a large effect on the world economy?

DISCUSS

3. Sometimes countries can put pressure on other countries by refusing to trade with them. Imagine you are part of a government committee that has to decide whether or not to trade with certain other countries. Discuss each of the cases below, and decide what you would do.

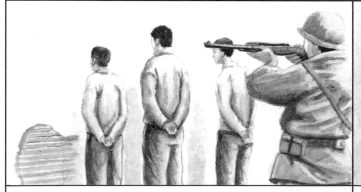

a. Reports of human rights abuses are reaching you from country 'A'. It is rumoured that the government there ordered the death of 50 political prisoners. You have a contract to provide ten ships to country 'A'. If you cancel the contract, hundreds of people in the UK will lose their jobs.

b. Country 'B' has just introduced a law banning people from practising a particular religion and has arrested a number of religious leaders. You are being urged to cut economic links with country 'B', but they are your main supplier of a particular type of computer component, which your computer industry needs urgently.

'Esperanto' is a devised language that supporters hoped would become an international language. Its use has never become popular and many people regard English as the international language.

KEY WORDS   world community   international pressure   international cooperation

c. You are about to sell weapons worth millions of pounds to country 'C'. You have just been informed that country 'C' has the worst health record of any country in its region and that infant death rates are rising there. The amount country 'C' is about to pay you for the weapons would pay for five new hospitals.

d. You are about to buy a large consignment of wood from country 'D', for a very reasonable price. This particular wood comes from an area of sustainable forest, but you know that country 'D' is also responsible for felling large areas of rainforest.

4. Write a declaration showing who you would and would not trade with if you had the power to decide. Your declaration could begin with 'We will not trade with countries that ...'

IMAGINE

5. Sometimes, political and economic solutions can be found to problems. Some Western governments have agreed to cancel some of the debts owed by Bolivia in exchange for the Bolivian Government's promise to introduce measures that will protect the rainforest. Imagine you have started a pressure group urging governments to work for economic and political solutions to world problems. Design your logo, and explain what your logo symbolises.

6. How would you reply to someone who says, "If we don't trade with them, someone else will."?

Objective
● To examine the implications of the world as an interdependent community in environmental and social terms.

A global community — environmental and social

BRAINSTORM

1. Brainstorm some things you do that might affect people thousands of miles away. The pictures below may give you some ideas.

COMPARE

2. Which of the things on your list are helpful and which are damaging to other people?

3. The conversation below has taken place on the Internet between Ricard, who is an environmental scientist, and people who have logged on to comment. Write replies from Ricard to Sarah, Shastri and Karl.

For a long time people believed the sea could be used as a rubbish dump. Anything pumped into the sea would be taken away from the coastline by currents and tides. This process cannot go on for ever. The Mediterranean and the North Sea are both polluted to dangerous levels. Governments and industry need to take a more responsible attitude.
Ricard – Canada

Pollution of the seas is inevitable. As world population grows, we produce more waste. Eventually, the whole planet will be poisoned. It's like a fish bowl – if you have a lot of fish in it, you have to clean it out.
Shastri – New Delhi

Water pollution may be a problem in some areas, but the oceans are so big, they will eventually dilute everything. We just need to pump the stuff further out.
Sarah – UK

Rich, industrialised countries should clean up their act, but what about poorer countries whose industries are just starting out? They can't afford to introduce expensive environmental programmes and it's not up to us rich countries to stop them from developing. **Karl – Germany**

In the 1950s and 1960s, in one small town in Japan, 45 people died and 76 others were seriously ill because of poisoned water caused by a factory.

KEY WORDS	pollution community environment interdependence

4. Read the story below. What could the happy ending to the story be?

CONSIDER

There was once a valley with steep sides – so steep that no one could ever climb in or out. Two tribes lived at either end of the valley. The first tribe were hunters. They stalked their prey in the woods and ate what they caught. The second tribe were farmers. They cleared land and grew their food. For many years, the two tribes lived without knowing of the existence of the other tribe. Gradually, their numbers increased. The hunters began to go further and further to catch their food, and the farmers had to clear more and more land for farming. One day, the two tribes met. "Why are you cutting down the trees that are home for our prey?" asked the hunters. "Why are you chasing your prey across our farms and damaging our crops?" asked the farmers. There are many endings to this story, but only one version ends happily for all.

5. The above story is a parable of the earth. The valley is our self-contained planet, and the tribes are the different nations of the world. Write a global version of the story. You could begin with the lines 'There was once a planet spinning in space. Many nations lived on the planet.' What would the global happy ending be?

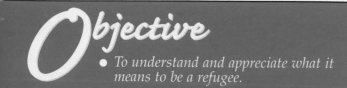

Objective

● To understand and appreciate what it means to be a refugee.

Refugees

1. The terms 'refugee' and 'displaced person' are often in the news. Read the definitions below to find out what they mean.

> A refugee is someone who has fled from their homeland and is unable to return there because of a real fear of persecution on the grounds of race, religion, nationality or political opinion.

> A displaced person is someone who has had to leave their homeland because of famine, war or disaster. Displaced persons are often called refugees but, strictly speaking, the two words mean different things.

CONSIDER

2. People sometimes believe that refugees in this country have chosen to come here to find a better life for themselves. The truth, for the vast majority of refugees, is that they have no choice. They would much rather stay in their own homes with their families and possessions, but they have had to flee in order to save their lives. Fourteen-year-old Said Abdi Said, a refugee from Somalia, says, "I know nobody wants refugees, but do they know that we don't want to be refugees?". How would you feel if you suddenly had to leave everything you owned and move to a completely different country? Apart from possessions, what would you miss most?

RESEARCH

3. In 1988, thousands of boys walked through Sudan towards Ethiopia. Many of the boys had been working as cattle herders when soldiers arrived. Chol was nine when this happened and he walked with hundreds of other boys from Wun Rog in Southern Sudan to the Ethiopian border near Tor. Find these places in an atlas and work out how far Chol walked, as the crow flies. Then read the comments he made five years later, below.

> We ate soil and the leaves of trees. After two months, we met people from the Anyak tribe who showed us how to catch and dry fish.

> In the day, the sun is hot and your feet burn — so we walked at night.

FACT TO THINK ABOUT ... FACT TO THINK ABOUT ... FACT TO THINK ABOUT ...

There are about 26 million refugees in the world today, and more than half of these are children.

KEY WORDS	refugee displaced person refugee camp

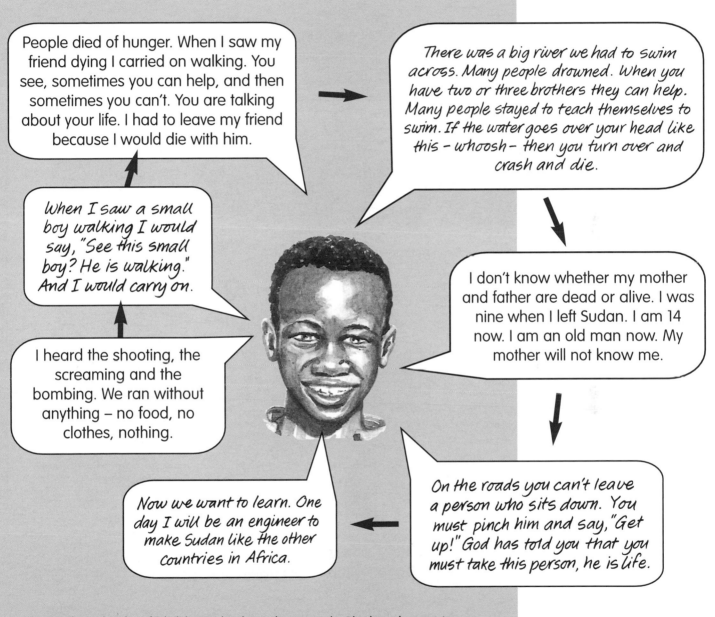

4. Many hundreds of children died on the march Chol took part in. Design a suitable memorial for the children who died. Write a commentary explaining what your memorial represents.

5. Imagine you have been told about a refugee family coming to live in your area. The family consists of mother, grandmother and three children aged twelve, seven and four. You have been given 50 pounds to put together a welcome box for the family. Plan what you would put in the box. You could begin with a map of the area showing schools, health centres, shops and other useful places.

PLAN

How can I contribute?

1. Make a list of the things you have done in the past year to help your school, local community, country or world. The pictures below may help to jog your memory:

2. Read the statements below. Give some other examples of knowledge, attitudes and action that help to make someone a good citizen.

Being a good citizen has three aspects – knowledge, attitudes and action.

Knowledge means finding out how your society works. For example, you need to know things like how the Government works, what laws are for and where you can get help for things.

FACT TO THINK ABOUT ... FACT TO THINK ABOUT ... FACT TO THINK ABOUT ...

Archbishop Desmond Tutu once said, "Let us create a society where people matter more than things."

KEY WORDS   community   citizen   society

Attitude is about your beliefs towards others. For example, a good citizen isn't racist or sexist, and they are interested in other people and their beliefs.

Action is about what you actually do. It can be small things like not dropping rubbish, or large things like running a youth centre or standing as a local councillor.

3. Copy and complete the chart below with things you could do that would help to make you a better citizen. Two boxes have been filled in as examples, but you should replace them with your own ideas.

	Knowledge	Attitudes	Action
Locally	Find out who my local councillor is.		
Nationally		My family say all southerners are 'posh'. I could think about this belief, where it comes from and whether or not it's true.	
Internationally			

4. As you get older, new opportunities will be open to you. Draw a picture of yourself as an adult, then surround the picture with suggestions of things you will do that will contribute to society.

5. What is a 'good citizen'? If everyone strove to be a good citizen, how would it affect the communities and world we live in?

CONSIDER

Choose one of these issues and decide what you could do to influence change.

Answers

NO HURRY
1 **a.** i   **b.** ii   **c.** ii   **d.** iii   **e.** iii

UNDERSTANDING HIV AND AIDS
1 **a.** True.
   b. True.
   c. False, the biggest group of people contracting the HIV virus in 1998 was babies, contracting the virus in the uterus or from breastfeeding.
   d. False, estimates suggest that ten million children have the virus worldwide.
   e. False, you can contract the virus from oral sex, although the chances of catching it this way are far lower than the risk of catching it from vaginal or anal sex.

2. HIV can be passed on this way: through vaginal or anal sex without a condom; through oral sex (but see note above); by sharing needles or syringes; from a mother to a baby during pregnancy, at birth or through breastfeeding.
   HIV cannot be passed on this way: by sharing cutlery; by sneezing on someone; by using the same flannel; from a blood transfusion in the UK – all blood and other tissue used for transfusions is screened for HIV and other viruses. This screening also applies in the majority of other countries. In the past, before HIV screening was introduced, some people were infected through blood transfusions.

THE COURT SYSTEM
3. The case of Ms A is criminal, Mr B is civil and Mr C could be both criminal and civil.

FINANCES AND LOCAL GOVERNMENT
1. All the services listed are provided by local government except the police. Police authorities are now independent, and the amount of council tax going to the police authority is listed separately on council tax bills. The fire service may also be run separately if its area covers more than one council, but in this case each council within that area will provide funding to the fire service from their budget.

MANAGING THE COUNTRY – FINANCES
1 **a.** Government revenue.
   b. Chancellor of the Exchequer.
   c. Government expenditure.
   d. Budget.
   e. Tax.

REFUGEES
3. Chol walked over 360 miles (580km).

© 2001 Folens Limited, on behalf of the authors.

United Kingdom: Folens Publishers, Apex Business Centre, Boscombe Road, Dunstable LU5 4RL.
Email: folens@folens.com

Ireland: Folens Publishers, Greenhills Road, Tallaght, Dublin 24.
Email: info@folens.ie

Poland: JUKA, ul. Renesansowa 38, Warsaw 01-905.

Eileen Osborne and Steph Yates hereby assert their moral rights to be identified as the authors of this work in accordance with the Copyright, Designs and Patents Act 1988.

Editor: Alison MacTier   Layout artist: James Brown
Cover design: Martin Cross
Illustrations: Kathy Baxendale, Jenny Gregory – Linda Rogers Associates, Debbie Riviere.
Photographs:
page 56 G Montgomery (left), Christa Stadtler (right), both Photofusion
page 76 Syndication International
page 77 Joanne O'Brien/Format
page 78 Adam Woolfitt/Robert Harding
page 79 Corbis Images
Text:
pages 72–73 Adapted extracts from *One Day We Had to Run* by Sybella Wilkes, published by Evans Brothers Ltd, 2A Portman Mansions, Chiltern Street, London W1U 6NR, Copyright © text Sybella Wilkes 1994. All rights reserved.

First published in 2001 by Folens Limited.
Reprinted 2001, 2002, 2003.

Every effort has been made to trace the copyright holders of material used in this publication. If any copyright holder has been overlooked, we should be pleased to make any necessary arrangements.

British Library Cataloguing in Publication Data. A catalogue record for this book is available from the British Library.

ISBN 1 84163 838-2